DIVINE
PEARLS

Spiritual Insight through Personal Short Stories

MARESHAH BROWN MILLER

ISBN 978-1-64416-865-3 (paperback)
ISBN 978-1-64416-866-0 (digital)

Christian Faith Publishing, Inc.
832 Park Avenue
Meadville, PA 16335
www.christianfaithpublishing.com

Printed in the United States of America

This collection of stories is dedicated to the loving memory of my dear husband, Kevin Anthony Miller. He always supported all my endeavors with encouragement, assistance, and an abundance of praise. Risking cliché overload, I can truly say Kevin was the wind beneath my wings; and even now, his love keeps lifting me higher.

ACKNOWLEDGEMENTS

To say I would not be who I am today without my parents is simply a fact. I am extremely thankful that my mom and dad gave me all the tools necessary to live a productive, creative, and love-filled life. They also gave me the treasured gift of family. The proverbial *village* was (is) the soil that nourished my creativity and love for relationship. Thank you to my dear sisters, grandmothers, aunts, uncles, cousins, nieces and nephews for the continuous appreciation and enthusiasm you have shown for my essays and stories.

My precious children, Ashley, Kortney, and Eddy, have graciously accepted that their experiences are shared with the world through my writing. Despite that, they are always excited to see what I will write next and they continue to encourage me with their love and support. Mostly, I am grateful that we continue to create joyful memories together.

I am blessed to have many friends who, over the years, have urged me to write and publish my work. I am thankful for friends who cheer for me and propel me to achieve my aspirations. A special thank you to my friend Joyce Beckford for her written review of this book and her consistent prayers.

With a heart of gratitude, I'm thankful to my pastors and mentors, Dr. Gary Smith and Dr. Janis Smith. Their spiritual guidance, example, encouragement and support for the past fifteen years have kept me grounded and inspired to pursue a genuine life. Thank you, Pastor Janis, for investing time and effort to endorse this book.

Thank you to the editors, illustrators, and graphic designers at Christian Faith Publishing for taking my ideas and bringing them to reality. And a special thank you to Matthew Brumbaugh for guiding me through my first publication experience.

CONTENTS

FOREWORD

I recently had a string of pearls repaired that my husband lovingly bought me twenty-five years ago. The strand had broken and was kept in a small cloth bag for eighteen years or so. The jeweler immediately recognized the pearls as authentic by their opalescence and glistening reflection underneath the examiner's bright light. I suppose most people would not recognize true pearls from fake ones, but the master jeweler cannot be fooled.

Mareshah has blessed our family for many years as a parishioner, choir member, and friend in the faith. She is a powerful woman of grace and determination. Her secret, without a doubt, is that she has discovered *The Pearl* of great price for herself. That is evident in the way she has journeyed through troubles, trials, and even losses. As a result, she is a true pearl in the hands of the expert jeweler. You will be blessed by her ability to share in a way that is comforting and inspirational. These vignettes will bring strength, tears, and joy when you feel weak and weary.

My strand of pearls has been through a lot of wear and tear, but today they are as beautiful as ever, after having been restored by the master jeweler.

Dr. Janis Smith
Co-Founder of City of Life Church
Kissimmee, FL

INTRODUCTION

Many people maintain a journal—some daily, and others weekly. I have done that a few times in my life, but never consistently. I believe one of the obstacles has been my poor penmanship. So, many years ago, I developed a habit. When I want to document a special moment or memory or record some specific revelation, I will sit at my computer and type. Then, I will ascribe a clever title. Over the years, I have shared some of these writings with family (and a few friends). However, sometimes these stories were written for my reference, reflection, and personal growth.

Divine Pearls is a collection of my personal short stories and reflections. Some will make you laugh, some will make you cry, but all will make you think. Each story is dated, but the writings are purposely not presented in chronological order. Although I would love to know that you devoured this book in one sitting, it is organized in such a way that you may enjoy each story separately.

My daddy was a storyteller. I grew up hearing stories of his island boyhood adventures, young adult sagas, and other special events that shaped his life. His stories always induced conversation and similar anecdotes from others. These story-telling sessions helped inform me of my heritage and connect me to my forefathers and foremothers. Stories capture the imagination and lay a foundation for teaching and learning. I hope my stories will inspire you to reflect on your life's journey and how you can mature as you walk towards your individual destiny; and in the process, *Divine Pearls* will construct a bridge for future generations.

Unless otherwise specifically stated, all Bible quotes are from the King James Version (KJV).

CHAPTER 1

MORE PLEASE . . .

April 13, 2018

Recently, my mind wandered back to 1992—when my husband, Kevin, worked in Nassau, Bahamas. The Bahamas was his native country, and he decided to accept a position as beverage director for the Crystal Palace Hotel. He would travel home every few weeks. This gave my daughters and me occasional opportunities to visit and enjoy the luxury of the hotel and the beauty of the Caribbean beaches. But for all practical purposes, it was as if I were a single mom of our daughters: four-year-old Ashley and three-year-old Kortney. We endured this lifestyle for two and one half years.

I worked a full-time paralegal job at a downtown law firm, but we lived in the suburbs. Fortunately, I worked for the managing partner, and he agreed to allow me to end my work day at four thirty each afternoon. Even so, after picking up my daughters from school and trudging through the Miami bumper-to-bumper rush-hour traffic, we would arrive home around six thirty in the evening.

Since it was just the three of us, I didn't add the stress of cooking elaborate meals during the week. My husband wasn't there. I figured it wasn't necessary. One of my favorite stops was an *all you can eat* Chinese buffet restaurant that Kevin had introduced me to a few years before. I would purchase one *to-go* meal for six dollars and fifty cents, and the girls and I would enjoy a delightful supper. Usually, we would have leftovers for the next day's dinner. You can't beat that! I wonder if that restaurant is still there; and if so, what would that same meal cost today?

Anyway, Kevin returned home permanently in 1994. Of course, the girls were ecstatic, and so was I. We resumed preparing home-cooked meals. Sometimes, I cooked. Other times, Kev cooked. Then one night, Kev asked the girls, "Do you want more?"

With widened bright eyes, Ashley shouted, "We can have more?!" It seemed that this was a more than pleasant revelation to her, as though the thought had never crossed her mind. Before that, the girls were quite content with eating their dinner and going about their nightly routine until bedtime. Now, their Daddy had introduced them to a whole new world of exploration—*eat as much food as you want.*

As the daughter of a Bahamian father and grand-daughter of paternal and maternal Bahamian grandparents,

I was raised understanding the island culture—you should always cook more than enough, so you will be able to offer a meal to anyone who may stop by or show up. And whoever visited, always left with a plate of food—you didn't take *no* for an answer. Food was the center of *community*; so I totally understood my husband's motives. In fact, I remember as a child my dad saying, "Let these children eat. That's why I work." I truly believe fathers find a lot of pleasure in knowing they can provide for their children. Knowing their children go to bed with a full belly makes them happy.

Well, a few months later, our very good friends invited our family to dinner at their Miami Beach home. They prepared an absolutely delicious pasta meal that we all thoroughly enjoyed. But, all of a sudden, Ashley politely asked, "May I have some more please?"

The host and hostess looked at each other with astonishment in their eyes. I could hear what they were thinking—*She's asking for more. There is no more.* Fully embarrassed, I felt like sliding under the table. That was my fault. I should have prepared my girls. I know every culture is different. I just didn't think about it. So, I quickly said, "She's fine. It's okay. She doesn't need anymore."

I could tell they felt badly about it. They brought out the dessert to deflect from that awkward moment, and we continued to enjoy the rest of the evening.

As I reminisced about this anecdote, I thought about how our Father God wants his children to be full of his Word. He said, "Blessed are those who hunger and thirst after righteousness, for they shall be filled" (Matthew 5:6). In essence, God has introduced the confessed Christian to a whole new world of exploration—the Bible (the Word of God). God is asking us the same question that Kev asked Ashley and Kortney —"Do you want more?"

After Ashley and Kortney realized they could ask for a second helping of food, from that point forward, they were never shy about asking for more. They embraced their new found liberty. David said in the Psalms, "O taste and see that the Lord is good" (Psalm 34:8). In another Psalm, David said that God's Word is sweeter than honey (Psalm 119:103). The prophet Jeremiah said to God, "When your words showed up, I ate them—swallowed them whole. What a feast!" (Jeremiah 15:16, MSG). The Word of God (the Bible) is the life blood of every Believer of Christ. "Man [mankind] shall not live on bread alone but on every word that comes from the mouth of God" (Matthew 4:4; Luke 4:4; Deuteronomy 8:3, NIV). Once we experience reading and absorbing the lessons from the Bible, we should crave its message and wisdom. So, when we ask, "May I have more please?" Our Father God doesn't look with astonishment. He whispers, "Yes, eat as much as you can, my child."

CHAPTER 2

TWO STRIKES!

October 1, 2006

On Saturday, September 30, 2006, my family headed to the bowling alley for a night of fun—and fun it was. Keep in mind, it had been years and years since I had even picked up a bowling ball; so of course, my daughters (Ashley and Kortney) figured this was going to be a night of *laughing at mom*. Well, to be truthful, it was.

To make the game more interesting, my daughters decided we should form teams—*young people against old people*. Translation—my husband, Kevin, and I against Kortney and Ashley's boyfriend, Eddy. Ashley decided to be the neutral player.

Well, I think everyone of us experienced a few gutter balls, but Eddy was the most experienced player and seemed to excel beyond the rest of us. Interestingly, we each had our own unique styles of getting that ball down the lane. Eddy would take a posture, using both hands, and roll the ball with effortless skilled technique. On the other hand, I was intrigued how Kortney would simply stroll to the line (taking great care not to break her expensive manicured fingernails) and calmly drop the ball on the lane. Sometimes, it went into the gutter; but most times, it went right where it needed to go. The most fascinating method (or lack thereof) was Ashley's. There was no concentration or style. She would arbitrarily throw the ball. One time, she would go in the gutter; and the next time, she would make a strike. In fact, she made the first strike of the night and more strikes than anyone else.

The *young people* got a big laugh from watching Kevin employ his technique with great skill and precision. He would study the lane and take great care in what position he stood and launch the ball down the lane like a pro bowler with style and poise. Guess what? Sometimes, he made a strike. Sometimes, he picked up a spare; but sometimes, he went in the gutter.

Now, as I told you earlier, I was in a category of my own. I simply was trying to figure out what I was doing. My ball went in the gutter the first couple of times. Kevin then wanted to try to give me instructions about what I was doing wrong. I quickly and calmly informed him that I was there to have fun. Well, I knocked down a few pins here and there, made a few more gutter balls, and was the brunt of many jokes that night. I simply laughed along with everybody else. I ended the first game with the lowest score, and Kevin and I lost that game. Of course, there was much gloating and teasing by the *young people;* but my favorite quote that night was, "Remember, slow and steady wins the race."

That quote was never truer than the night of September 30. Toward the end of the second game, Kortney bragged to Eddy, "Don't worry, they can't catch us. We got this in the bag."

Well, what do you know? On the tenth (last) round, I bowled a strike, which meant I got an additional turn. I then proceeded to knock down several pins and picked up the spare. Kortney's exact words were, "I didn't know you had it like that!"

With Kev bowling his usual good game, we came from behind at the last minute and won the game! Everyone was surprised, and I was shocked. I couldn't stop laughing. "I told you, slow and steady wins the race" I kept repeating. All of a sudden, I felt more confident.

We had just enough time for a third game. Of course, we had to break the tie. Things went along pretty much as usual. However, I was bowling a little better than before. Then about round six, without warning, I bowled a strike. But wait—round seven, I bowled another strike! Two strikes back to back! Who would have thought! No one else bowled two strikes together that night. Me—the most inexperienced of them all—bowled two strikes in a row; and Kevin and I went on to win that game. The *old people* were the winners for the night!

"The first shall be last, and the last shall be first."[1] Weren't these the words of our Lord, Jesus Christ? The crowd had counted me out. I wasn't even in the running. I was considered no threat. After all, I didn't have the skill or the technique, poise, or experience. Think about it—these are the same lies Satan thinks and says about you. He uses people to tell you that you don't have what it takes to win this Christian race. He points to the fact that your score is low right now. Seems like no matter how much you do, you end up in the gutter. Sometimes, you do things right; and then the next day, you find yourself doing what you know you shouldn't be doing. The enemy of your soul tells you how bad you are, and that you'll never get it right. He doesn't take you seriously. He thinks you are a big joke. On top of that, somebody comes along to tell you that you must do it just like them to be successful; and it doesn't work. And besides, nobody has the patent to the successful Christian life. Remember, all of us had a different technique when bowling, but everybody went in the gutter at some point.

Well, God's translation for *slow and steady wins the race* is, "Not by might, nor by power, but by my [God's] Spirit."[2] It won't be your technique, and it won't be your skill; but as long as you don't give up, and you stay in the race, you will win the race and defeat Satan by the grace of God, the Spirit God, and the Word of God. When Satan least expects it, you'll make a strike; and when he thinks he can

---

[1] Matthew 19:30; Matthew 20:16
[2] Zechariah 4:6

sneak back and overtake you, you will hit him again with the strength of the Word by the grace of God.[3] No matter what people around you say or your circumstances may lead you to believe, remember that God declares through his Word that you are more than a conqueror.[4] That means you don't just win—you excel! Then Satan will most certainly have to say, "I didn't know she/he had it like that."

I'm reminded that Satan thought that he had won when Jesus died on the cross. He and his gang threw a party; but when Satan wasn't looking, Jesus got up from the grave with life and power—STRIKE ONE![5] Then he empowered His church by the Holy Spirit to evangelize and disciple the world—STRIKE TWO![6] If we equate this analogy to baseball, there's one strike left; and the devil will be OUT! It's coming. We already know he's out. We don't have to wonder about that. Jesus is going to burst the eastern sky, take his children home (heaven), and bind Satan forever!—STRIKE THREE![7] So, don't worry that things don't seem to be looking positive or going your way right now. You're on Jesus' team. You WIN!

---

[3] Ephesians 6:10-17
[4] Romans 8:35-39; Revelation 2:10, 25-29
[5] Matthew 28:5-7; Mark 16:5-7; Luke 24:3-9
[6] Acts 2:1-47
[7] Rev. 20:1-15

CHAPTER 3

DADDY'S WORD

Jesus said, "Heaven and earth shall pass away, but my word shall not pass away" Mathew 24:35 (KJV).

A Father's Day Tribute
June 19, 2009

I grew up in Miami, Florida. But many people don't realize that the city of Miami is one small urban area, and that Dade County consists of many townships that spread far and wide around the city of Miami. So technically, I should probably say that I grew up in Richmond Heights. And my grandmother, aunts, and uncles lived in the next town, which is Perrine.

Why am I explaining all of this? Well, I'm remembering today a story that happened when I was a little girl. One summer day, my dad asked, "Who wants to go to Perrine?"

Actually, we had a very unique pronunciation for that township. We would say, "Pea-rine." My two sisters and I (there were only three of us then) immediately yelled with excitement, "Meeeee! I do!" For us, going to Pea-rine was the ultimate adventure at that time in our lives.

So we each slid into our rubber flip flop sandals. (Dad always took us to the Army and Navy store and let us each pick out a pair of flip flops at the beginning of summer. I think that's how we knew summer had begun. This was probably the second best adventure. Obviously, it didn't take much to please us.) Anyway, we hopped in the back seat of Dad's car (which was probably a Chevrolet, Cadillac, or Pontiac). There were no seat belts back then. We were giddy with anticipation about going to Pea-rine. Dad backed out of the yard, and off we went.

Daddy made a few stops. I don't remember exactly where we went—most likely the Army and Navy store and a hardware store. Then we were back in the car to fulfill our great adventure. However, we noticed that we were on the road that led back to our house. Suddenly, Dad turned to the mysteriously quiet back seat to see all three of us with tears streaming down our faces. He asked us what was wrong. With great sadness and distraught in our voices, we sobbed, "You said we were going to Pea-rine!"

Dad said, "We did go to Pea-rine." After a while, Dad realized that we equated going to Perrine with going to my grandmother's house (my maternal grandmother). As far as we were concerned, if we didn't go to Grandma's house, we had not gone to Perrine. Needless to say, this was a real chuckle for Dad. He understood our heartbreak, but he had done what he promised.

How many times have we done this with God? Taken one or more of his promises and put our own little twists on it. The Word of God is the most solid, firm, truthful, unchanging thing that exists in heaven and on earth; but if we are not careful, we will read God's Word out of context and receive a distorted view of what God said. Daddy said he was taking us to Perrine, and he did. It wasn't his fault that we had a distorted view of what was Perrine. That was our own doing (shaped by our experiences). Daddy didn't go to Grandma's house, but Daddy kept his word because he never promised us Grandma's house.

It's the same way with God. Scripture says, "But my God shall supply all of your need according to his riches in glory by Christ Jesus" (Philippians 4:19). Most people use this scripture to insinuate that God will arbitrarily look down from heaven and spontaneously give us everything we want. Others may take a more conservative view and say, "Well, God's not going to let me go hungry, and he will provide my food and shelter." But if you look at the context of that scripture (read the verses before it and after it), Paul was commending the church members at Philipi for their faithfulness in sacrificial giving to Paul's ministry and to help the work of God continue. Here is part of what he said to them first. "No church entered into partnership with me in giving and receiving, except you only. Even in Thessalonica you sent me help for my needs once and again. Not that I seek the gift, but I seek the fruit that increases to your credit. I have received full payment and more. I am well supplied having received from Epaphroditus the gifts you sent, a fragrant offering, a sacrifice acceptable, and pleasing to God" (Philippians 4:14–18, ESV). If we are stingy people, we really don't have the right to expect God to do too much in our lives. Then we can't sit back and cry and say God didn't keep his Word.

Now, there was certainly nothing wrong with us wanting to go to Grandma's house. I'm sure if we had asked Daddy, he would have taken us; but because we had a distorted view of what he already said, we didn't ask. God is not a man, that he should lie; . . . hath he said and shall he not do it? Or hath he spoken and shall he not make it good (Numbers 23:19)? Abba Father's Word is true, but let's make sure that we understand what he said.

CHAPTER 4

THE SEA OF MERCY

March 1, 2007

"If I were God, I would destroy this world!" Have you ever said those words or a set of words arranged in a similar fashion? Well, that's why we're not God! That, in itself, is a blessing. The truth is, this world warrants destruction. Every one of us has *blown it* so many times. In fact, when Adam messed up and defied God in the Garden of Eden, God could have just wiped out everything and started over; but he didn't. There's a reason for that—a reason that we, in our humanness, don't fully understand. The Psalmist, David, states it like this: "His [God] mercy endureth forever" (Psalm 136). In other words, no matter how many times we mess up, God has another ounce of mercy to dispense towards us. He forgives the unforgivable. He is a God of second chance, third chance, fourth chance, one millionth chance! God—never—gives—up—on—us!

On February 10, 2007, this truth of God's mercy came alive for me much more than it ever had before. That morning, I rushed my husband, Kevin, to the hospital emergency room because of chest pains and heart attack symptoms. My husband has a history of heart trouble since the year 2001, so we weren't taking any chances that morning by ignoring the symptoms. After initial examination and tests, the doctors determined that Kevin had two arteries that were 90 percent (90%) blocked, and he would have to receive an angioplasty. This is modern heart surgery where there is no invasive incision. A special tube is weaved through the artery via the groin, and a stint (small tube) is implanted in the artery to keep it open for blood flow. This would make the fourth time Kevin would undergo this procedure.

Why did I think of God's mercy on this particular morning? There are many reasons. First of all, up until the moment of the pain, Kevin was walking around, working, feeling fine, unaware that he had two arteries that were 90 percent blocked. Only God could make that happen. Secondly, with that much blockage, he was primed for a heart attack; but he didn't have one. In fact, he's never had one. Also, keep in mind that Kevin had had several previous angioplasty surgeries—the odds were against him! But the one thing that plunged me into deep thought about the depth of God's mercy is my husband's lifestyle and actions. In 2001, after Kevin's first angioplasty, I was present as the doctor wheeled him out of the operating room and stated these words: "Mr. Miller, if you want to see your daughters walk down the aisle, no more smoking or drinking" (habits he embraced after we married).

One would think that those words wouldn't have to be spoken or deliberated at all. For me, the comment would be an obvious conclusion considering the circumstances. However, not only did my husband continue those habits, he continued to eat poorly; and now we sit in 2007 in, yet another hospital awaiting another surgery. Need I say, "If it were me, I would have said forget this guy. He's not trying to help himself; just let him die." Miraculously, God obviously didn't say that! To be clear, I didn't want anything to happen to my husband. I just wanted him to change his habits, so he would not suffer a heart attack.

Of course, I've witnessed God's mercy many times before that February Saturday morning. There was the time my mother had colon surgery and couldn't be revived from the anesthesia. It seemed hopeless to most, but God had mercy and heard the prayers of his people. Then in 1996, mom endured a similar fate after being struck by a city garbage truck. After a hip replacement surgery, the effect of anesthesia was even more severe; and she was in a coma for over a week. Ministers walked out shaking their heads and saying their goodbyes; but my sisters and I called upon God, who had mercy. Mom is still here with us today enjoying abundant life. My family and I could never forget the Hurricane Andrew of 1992, when we were all stuffed into two bathrooms trying to hold the doors shut as the roof threatened to peel away from the walls. We prayed and prayed, and God had mercy. Of course, the day that God reached down into my young life and said, "I forgive you, Mareshah, enter into my kingdom." Also, I think about the many times I said I would pray, but didn't—tried to stop a habit, but couldn't—should have told someone about Jesus, but wouldn't. God didn't throw in the towel on me. He extended his mercy.

I am in awe of my God! He seems to be able to teach me in every situation. He uses every circumstance and phase of my life to reveal himself to me and help me mature to become more like his son, Jesus. God doesn't give up on people. People give up on people. God's mercy is so vast. It never runs out. He has enough for everybody everyday—FOREVER! (Lamentations 3:21–23).

Epilogue
May 7, 2018

After that February operation, Kevin stopped drinking and smoking. By the way, he never smoked in front of me or the girls. Somehow, he thought he was hiding it from Ashley and Kortney, but they told me they knew. He had a couple more angioplasty surgeries after 2007, but he always bounced back quickly, not missing a beat.

Kevin enjoyed his life. He did not allow a heart condition to control his pursuit of all life had to offer. He worked hard doing what he loved—managing restaurants. He also enjoyed working in our yard planting and maintaining a garden and fruit trees and interacting and sharing with our neighbors. He went fishing and even played golf when possible. In 2010, he walked Ashley down the aisle on her wedding day—one of the proudest moments of his life. However, on December 11, 2014—while in the midst of a stress test in his cardiologist's office—Kevin died. The professionals went to work immediately and revived him within forty-five seconds. They transported him to the hospital across the street. The next day, he went to surgery, where a defibrillator/pacemaker was implanted in his heart. Doctors had been asking Kevin to have this surgery for years, but he resisted. Now, he had no choice.

Kevin was released from the hospital a few days after surgery, but this time was different. He did not bounce back so quickly. He never seemed to be comfortable with the pacemaker. On the morning of February 4, as I traveled to work, my cell phone rang. I knew it would be Kev on the other end. We usually left home around the same time each morning and would make that one last call to each other before we started our work day. However, I answered to a panicked, Kevin screaming, "I'm in trouble! I'm in trouble!"

I began asking him, "Where are you?! Where are you?!" A few seconds later, a paramedic got on the phone and explained that Kevin had exited the Florida Turnpike and called 911. He told me he and the other paramedics were working on him at that moment and transporting him to the hospital emergency room. I got a lump in my chest as big as a baseball. I began to pray and called family as I drove to the hospital. As I traveled, I received a call from the hospital chaplain telling me I needed to get to the hospital as soon as possible. My heart sank. As much as I didn't want to believe it, in my heart, I knew. My Kev left me that day for a better home (heaven). Even on that day, God's mercy was at work. God allowed Kevin to pull off the Turnpike, and no one else was hurt or killed. God allowed Kevin to call me, so I would know what was happening.

Life is still strange without him, but I know he would want me to live. Kev enjoyed eight fulfilling years after my initial writing. He never allowed his heart condition to be a factor in how he enjoyed life. I believe he knew his time was up. The week before he died, he brought me a beautiful bouquet of roses. I asked him what was the occasion.

He answered, "You deserve them. You have been through a lot, and I want you to know I love you."

The night before he passed away, he bought my mom a box of sugar free chocolates in a heart-shaped box. He did that every year for Valentine's Day. I almost said to him, "It's not Valentine's Day yet. Why did you buy them now?" But I decided to say nothing. Mom and I later realized that Kev was giving us our Valentine's Day gifts because he knew he would not be here. Ironically, we laid Kev to rest on Valentine's Day.

Kev and I cherished thirty years of marriage. We shared good times and bad, ups and downs; but he told me at least ten times each day, "I love you." Life is still strange without him, but I know he would want me to live—by God's mercy.

CHAPTER 5

LOST

May 1, 2018

Recently, I noticed a few pairs of sunglasses laying around my house. I have no doubt that they belong to my eldest daughter, Ashley. Keeping track of her sunglasses appears to be one of her little challenges in life. One Sunday, when she and her husband, Eddy, were visiting me, she seemed perplexed and then stated she was looking for her sunglasses. Eddy then replied with a chuckle. "They're on top of your head." We all got a good laugh out of this scenario. I believe I said something to the effect of, "You're too young for this type of episode." Her sunglasses were right there—attached to her—but she couldn't see them.

This catapulted me back to a time when Ashley was two years old and my youngest, Kortney, was six months old. Prior to this publication, I think I shared this story only with my husband, Kevin, and my sisters. It's only recently that I told Ashley and Kortney. One Saturday, Kortney was asleep in her crib in my room; and I decided I would take a rare opportunity to get a nap. Ashley was very independent and good about entertaining herself and staying out of trouble. I felt she would be fine, so I ventured off into my rest.

A couple hours later, I awoke feeling revived. I immediately went to look for Ashley. I expected her to be either right there in the room with me or in the living room, but she was not in either place. I went into her bedroom, but she was not there. I checked the third bedroom. Now, I started to panic. I ran through every room in the house—bathrooms, kitchen, closets. No matter where I looked, I could not find my child! Now, I'm hysterical. The front door was locked and the chain was on, so there was no possible way she could have gotten outside; but I ran outside anyway. I remember at that moment, I threw up my hands and yelled, "God help me!"

I ran back into my bedroom, and there spotted Ashley laying on the other side of my bed on the carpet sound asleep. She and Kortney were both resting peacefully; but now, I was a nervous wreck. Even though I had found her, I was still unnerved. Every ounce of serenity that was yielded from that nap had been quickly mutilated. As a result, without exaggeration, Ashley was ten years old before I allowed myself another restful sleep (day or night). In retrospect, abandoning my personal rest was an extreme response to a one-time incident; but that's what I did.

But the point I am making is that Ashley was right there the entire time—in the same room with me; but I didn't see her. I exerted a lot of energy and emotions need-lessly. How many times are we looking for answers in life? The answers are staring us in the face, but we just can't see them.

For example, I remember the story of Moses from the Bible. He led thousands of people (the Israelites) out of Egypt and away from a government that oppressed and enslaved them. However, Pharaoh and his army pursued these people to take them back to Egypt. As a result, the Israelites found themselves facing a vast ocean (the Red Sea) while an army was chasing them. There appeared to be absolutely no possibility that they would escape. Needless to say, that was a much more significant dilemma than trying to locate sunglasses. However, the principle still applies. "Then the Lord said to Moses why are you crying out to me? Tell the Israelites to move on. Raise your staff and stretch out your hand over the sea to divide the water so that the Israelites can go through the sea on dry ground."

This quote reveals that Moses had the method for solv-ing the problem right in his hand, but he didn't realize it. After Moses stretched his rod towards the Red Sea, God divided the waters; and the Israelites successfully crossed and escaped the army (Exodus 14:15–22, NIV). Moses was praying for an answer, but God basically told Moses that he was holding the answer right in his hand.

As we encounter life's predicaments, we should settle down and ask God to enhance our vision (insight, intu-

ition, discernment) (James 1:5). Whether we are just perplexed or full blown hysterical, **God helps us overcome
being oblivious to the obvious (or not so obvious).**

CHAPTER 6

"Train Up A Child..."

(My *"Yes Ma'am"* Saga)
June 17, 2012

"Train up a child in the way he should
go, and when he is old, he will not depart
from it."

(Proverbs 22:6)

"Did you have a nice Christmas?"

"Yes."

"Yes Ma'am. You should answer, 'Yes Ma'am.'"

This is probably a familiar scenario for most of us who
grew up in the southern region of the United States or the
Caribbean Islands. Honestly, I didn't have to be corrected
much because it came very naturally to me as a young girl
growing up in Miami, Florida. The daughter of an African-
American mother and a Bahamian father, I was taught

(probably before I could talk) to say, "Yes Ma'am," "Yes, Sir," and "No Ma'am," "No Sir" to adults—any adult. This was good manners and a sign of respect. So to this day, I still do it. I'm a living testament to King Solomon's advice which we hear quoted so much—"Train up a child in the way he should go, and when he is old, he will not depart from it." Or in my case, *she.*

Interestingly, when I was rearing my daughters, I taught them to say *yes* and *no.* Subconsciously, I thought the term *Yes Ma'am* was a residual from slavery and not really necessary. I never voiced this to anyone—not even to myself. I certainly never expressed this to my daughters. I simply taught them to say *yes* and *no.* However, I was sure to emphasize what was not acceptable. *Yeah, uh huh,* and *nope* where never acceptable, especially when addressing adults; and shaking your head in place of a verbal response was absolutely unacceptable. They learned and quickly implemented what they were taught. "Train up a child in the way she should go, and when she is old, she will not depart from it."

I didn't realize that this simple decision would prove to be controversial throughout my daughters' lives. They would occasionally be corrected, and other children who used the phrase would be perceived to be more respectful than they. Of course, my girls meant no disrespect. They simply had not been taught that; and after a certain age, a person doesn't just develop that habit. "Train up a child in the way she should go, and when she is old, she will not depart from it." I personally see no disrespect in saying,

"Yes," instead of, "Yes Ma'am," but for my children's sake, I wish I had taught them to say, "Yes Ma'am"—one less issue for them to deal with. And more importantly, my daughters would be vehicles to perpetuate respect.

What makes this discussion just that more interesting is that while my daughters are saying *yes* and *no*, I address my elders with, "Yes Ma'am" and "No Ma'am." In fact, as I previously stated, I still use the term today and probably will until I leave earth. "Train up a child in the way she should go, and when she is old, she will not depart from it."

As a school teacher, I expect respect from my students. However, a respectful yes or no will do. But surprisingly, I hear "Yes Ma'am" more often than I expect. I have observed that usually it comes from an African-American child because it is intrinsic to the culture. "Train up a child in the way he should go, and when he is old, he will not depart from it."

I recall a time when I was supervisor of several legal secretaries in a law firm. This was around 1990–1991. I was in my early thirties, and Mickey (one of the secretaries) was in her mid to late forties. Mickey would always address me with, "Yes Ma'am." One day, I said, "Mickey, stop saying 'Yes Ma'am' to me. You are older than I am. If anything, I should say 'Yes Ma'am' to you."

Mickey said, "I know. I can't help it. It was the way I was raised."

"Train up a child in the way she should go, and when she is old, she will not depart from it."

Why am I making much of this small phrase? My Mickeys have multiplied! Almost every department store, supermarket, restaurant, church activity, even family gatherings! "Yes Ma'am… Yes Ma'am… Yes Ma'am… Yes Ma'am." They are addressing me! One Saturday afternoon, I texted my daughters and husband, "If one more person in their thirties and forties says Yes Ma'am to me, I'm going to scream!" This was met with a couple of LOLs and an encouraging text from my husband about how beautiful and intelligent I am and how those people just are showing me respect. Thankfully, he always knows just the right words to say.

What do I take away from all this? In an era where we think all that is honorable is lost, it's encouraging to realize that RESPECT is still sought and given. More than that—respect is obviously still being taught. I cheated my girls out of this little part of their heritage. Now, if I scorn the *Yes Ma'ams* that come my way, I would only continue to chip away at something that is purer than I first imagined. I probably will still cringe when that forty-year-old person says "Yes Ma'am" to me, but I won't stop them from saying it. I guess I'm a testament to another of King Solomon's principles—"Happy is the man [woman] that finds wisdom and gets understanding" (Proverbs 3:13, KJV)

CHAPTER 7

GENERATIONS

We Can Make Our Past a Prison or a Pedestal
April 15, 2003

Have you ever thought about all of the *begats* of the Bible and why they are there? (Adam begat Seth . . . Seth begat Enos, etc. (Genesis 5). Yes, I know that it was important for God to mark the lineage of his chosen people and connect the line of Judah to the birth of Jesus Christ; and those records also help us understand some of what is going on in the world today. But I also believe people have an inborn desire to know where they come from. How does one explain the burning curiosity of adopted children about their birth parents, even when they have wonderful adoptive parents? It is part of our emotional makeup to embrace our roots. Included in that plan was the fact that earlier generations would pass on to the next generation a solid foundation for a good, peaceful, and prosperous life. As evidence, we see that God continuously demands his children to do just that. The sixth chapter of Deuteronomy is only one of many places in the Bible where God commands his people to teach and nurture their children in the ways of God. Throughout Proverbs, the wise man, Solomon, constantly admonishes young people to listen to their parents. The Psalmist, David, wrote songs about sharing the goodness of God with each generation. In fact, among the people of Israel, passing of the baton was evident in the fact that people from a certain tribe were trained to do a certain job. I don't think there's any mistake here. The earlier generation is expected to pour into the next generation. This is what keeps the world functioning.

The question becomes, "What's being passed on to the next generation?" If wisdom, righteousness, morality, goodness, and all the things that fall in line with those virtues are being passed on, we have no problem. Unfortunately, because of the sinful nature of mankind, this ideal falls short most of the time. Too often, we give the next generation baggage they were never meant to carry; and the next generation adds a few more pieces to pass down the line. Perhaps, you remember a man name Jacob. His very name meant *trickster*. He lived up to it well. He successfully tricked his father into blessing him with the inheritance that is designated for the first-born son. Esau was Jacob's older twin brother, and by tradition, should have received the blessing. Now look closely and understand that Jacob was only one in a long line of deceivers. Abraham was Jacob's grandfather. Before Abraham had any children, he convinced his wife Sarah to conspire with him and make King Abimelech believe that Sarah was Abraham's sister and not his wife because he was afraid that Abimelech might kill him to get Sarah. God intervened and put an end to the deceit, but Abraham's actions almost cost the destruction of a man and his family (Genesis 20). Later, Abraham and Sarah had a son named Isaac. When Isaac grew up and married, he went to live in a city where once again King Abimelech reigned. Isaac did the same thing his father Abraham had done years before. He presented his wife, Rebekah, as his sister because he was afraid the men of the city would kill him to get his wife (Genesis 26). Then Isaac and Rebekah had this son (Jacob) who had, no doubt, observed his parents engaging in deceitful deeds. Don't forget that Jacob's mother, Rebekah, was the one who constructed the plan for Jacob to steal Esau's inheritance.[8] If you look further into her family life, you will see the same lifestyle. Jacob later goes to live with Rekah's brother, Laban, and agrees to work for seven years for the privilege of marrying Laban's daughter, Rachel. However, on the day of Jacob's wedding, Laban snuck his older daughter, Leah, into Jacob's bed, sealing a marriage with Leah instead of Rachel; so Jacob had to work another seven years to marry Rachel (Genesis 29). Rebekah and Laban obviously grew up among deceivers. But it doesn't stop with Jacob. He later had a strong encounter with God, who changed his name to Israel. Eventually, Jacob (Israel) *begat* twelve sons. Ten of them conspired to get rid of Jacob's favorite son named Joseph by selling him into slavery. Then they smeared animal's blood on Joseph's coat and made Jacob believe for

---

[8] Although God had already said that Jacob would be the line by which the generations would be blessed, God did not need Jacob's deceit to make this happen; as always, God took man's mess and used it for his glory. God could have accomplished this without Jacob and Rebekah's help.

almost twenty years that Joseph was dead. Can you see the big picture yet? The deceit continued from generation to generation.

On the other hand, sometimes, we open ourselves up to a lifestyle, a way of living, or a habit that was not passed on to us by our ancestors. In our own pursuit of life, we take on things which are then passed on to our children, grandchildren, and great-grandchildren. For instance, David, the *man after God's own heart*. This man loved God; yet in his weakness, he knowingly took another man's wife, impregnated her, and then tried to cover up his deeds by having the man killed. I don't think it can get any worse than that. However, being confronted with his sin by the prophet, David confessed and pleaded for forgiveness. God forgave David, but his deeds brought a price to pay by his family. God said, "The sword shall never depart from thine house." David messed up his family. His son, Amnon, raped his daughter, Tamar. David's son, Absalom, killed Amnon (premeditated murder) because of the rape. Absalom wanted nothing to do with his father because he did nothing about the rape. Absalom later raped his father's wife in public. Then Absalom fought to take control of David's kingdom and ended up dead in the process (2 Samuel 11–17). Another son, Adonijah, also tried to take over David's kingdom (1 Kings 1). Even David's son, Solomon (the wisest man), was affected. He eventually was the next king, but he too had a woman issue. He had seven hundred wives and three hundred mistresses, and they led him away from God. This had a ripple-down effect on the generations that followed (1 Kings 11). David passed a legacy of sexual immorality and murder. His sons did not have to accept this into their lives, but they did.

Keep in mind, these are our forefathers of the faith: Abraham, Isaac, Jacob, David. These people knew God, but they failed to close the door on those generational curses. There, I've said it. Some want to pretend there's no such thing. Paul refers to them as *strong holds*. You don't have to even look to the Bible. Just look at your own life. We all have something to look at. What habit, or situation, or lifestyle did your parents dwell in that you now find yourself dwelling in? What demonic devices did you open yourself to and now notice that your children are struggling with the same demons? Lying, gluttony, alcoholism, drugs, arrogance, fear, pornography, promiscuity, passivity, anger, self-indulgence, procrastination, co-dependency, laziness— just to name a few. The good news is that we are not bound to doom. First, we must be honest with ourselves and our children. We can't live in denial. How can God fix what we don't admit is broken? Then we have to stand up and show the devil the bloodline of Jesus Christ. Afterwards, we must turn away from whatever it is that's trying to hold us captive. If this means confronting someone, then it must be done. We must put on the whole armor of God that we can stand against the tricks of the devil, and we must pray constantly (Ephesians 6:11–18). If necessary, don't be afraid to seek professional Christian counseling. The bottom line is this: **We can make our past a prison or a pedestal.**

We can stew in self-pity or blame our parents for our suffering; but this will only keep us bound. At best, we can identify the problem and lay it at the feet of Jesus—cry out and let God pull us up. We can use the thing that wants to control us as a stepping stone to restoration. According to Paul, this struggle that we have is not natural. It is spiritual. We are mighty through God to pull down those strong holds (2 Corinthians 10:4). We must begin to recognize the magnitude of power that we hold within us. We have the power of the blood of Christ, the power of the Word of God, and the power of the Holy Spirit. God is able to do exceedingly, abundantly, above, all that we ask or think according to the power that works in us (Ephesians 3:20). For some, this will be an immediate deliverance. For others, it will be a battle while being held up by grace on one side and truth on the other. Yes, we are more than conquerors through Jesus Christ (Romans 8:39). Amen.

Now beloved, since we have been strategically positioned as a link between the past and the future, let us bless our children in words and deeds; and remember—no matter what we say, it is what we do that has the greatest impact on the next generation.

CHAPTER 8

LOOK FORWARD AND MARCH!

Mount Up and Soar!
12341234123412341234123412341234

May 15, 2003

I press toward the mark for the prize of
the high calling of God in Christ Jesus.
—Philippians 3:14

What are you doing? Or not? Be fruitful and multiply (Genesis 1:22). Tell Pharaoh to let my people go (Exodus 8). Go to Nineveh and preach (Jonah 1:2). Go into all the world and preach the gospel to every creature (Mark 16:15; Matthew 28:19). From the beginning of time, God has been telling people to move forward and accomplish. Accomplish what? That is a question that seems to be asked in a bubble. Some are sitting and waiting for life to happen to them, being tossed like leaves in the wind; no purpose; no destination; no control. That was never God's plan for people. He gave us dominion over the earth and told us to pursue and conquer. However, in order to know when to move and how to move, we have to be connected to the great orchestrator, who is God. When we are not connected, we either sit in fear and do nothing or rage ahead in haste and make a big mess. Isaiah poetically states it when he says, "They that wait upon the Lord shall renew their strength. They shall mount up with wings as eagles. They shall run and not be weary, and they shall walk and not faint" (Isaiah 40:31). And may I add—**they shall look forward and march.**

Our destiny is heaven, but the road traveled resides on earth. There are things to be accomplished. God never meant for us to be a tumbleweed. He expects us to have vision and act upon it. The formula for initiative and success is explained in chapter 1 of Psalms. People who seek Godly counsel and meditate on God's Word shall be wise, strong, and prosperous; but ungodly people are like the chaff tossed in the wind. Chaff is the unusable part of grain that is thrown away or blown away. This is how some people live—tossed around by whatever happens next. "The steps of a good man [person] are ordered by the Lord, and he delights in his ways" (Psalm 37:23).

Stir up the gift that is within you—the Holy Spirit (2 Timothy 1:6). He will enable you to activate the other gifts and talents that God has given you. What you deem small, God multiplies for his glory and your benefit.

Sometimes we may not see the fruit (results) in our lifetime. Jeremiah preached to a defiant set of people, who never seemed to heed Jeremiah's messages; but after Jeremiah was dead and gone, Daniel read the writings of Jeremiah and used them as tools to help him look forward and march (Daniel 9:2–3). As we examine the life—memories, conquests, defeats, virtues, and flaws of our ancestry—let's use them as fuel for vision and energy for marching, mounting, and soaring. Yes, there are times to stand still; and there are times to move forward. So stay connected to the great choreographer so you'll know when to do both and continue on a pace forward; never backwards.

Remember, your barometer of measurement should always be through spiritual eyes. Your and God's view of success and progressiveness will not be the same as the world's view. When we encounter what we consider to be setbacks, we must look at what God may be doing in the larger scheme of things. At the end of it all, the lives touched and the impact made on people encountered will tell the story.

From preteen to grandparent, you may identify with one or more of these situations: You're called to be a lawyer, but you shy away because you're too lazy to study. You have the makings of a doctor, but fear keeps you from trying. God told you to stay on a job, but you let pride and conflict with your boss go against what God said, so you leave. Can you showcase original drawings and art across the world but refuse to break out of your secluded environment and take chances? Could you possibly be a world-renowned praise dancer but are too lazy to practice or won't live a holy life so the anointing can rise to its full potential in you? Perhaps, you have the makings of a future politician but refuse to read and broaden your horizons. You have a natural talent but just keep using it on a small scale and refuse to let yourself dream big dreams. You feel a tug of compassion to volunteer at the health center or soup kitchen, but it is easier to just watch TV all day. Maybe you have an opportunity to teach young people to sew, crochet, or play an instrument; but you would rather go shopping in all your spare time. You got an idea to start a business, but you never acted upon it, or you started it and threw in the towel after one setback. You go to concert after concert or seminar after seminar. Have you implemented anything that was taught? You work on an hourly-wage job and are satisfied with getting your paycheck every two weeks and have not given one thought to future goals. God told you that you are (you fill in the blank), but you don't let your mind conceive it. Yet some person or people in your life told you or made you feel that you are nothing, and you chose to believe them, so you do nothing.

By now, I'm sure some of you are saying that I spiritualize everything. When you have lived more than a few years on this earth, you will come to understand that **everything is spiritual.** What are you doing? Or not?

CHAPTER 9

FINISH!

Completing What We Start
August 15, 2003

Noah finished the ark. Solomon finished the temple.
Nehemiah finished the wall. What have you finished?

During the first year of high school, my elder daughter, Ashley, was a color guard. For those who may not know, color guards are the flag performers you see during half-time at the high school and college football games. (Don't feel bad. I didn't know at first.) Well, Ashley knew before she even reached high school that she wanted to be a color guard. She gave up her summer to attend practices (guard camp); and when school opened, it was an exciting time for her.

One day, when I picked up Ashley after practice, I could see that she was upset before she even got in the car. Upset is probably not an adequate word. My usually calm, laid back, nothing-bothers-me daughter was physically shaken and had fire in her eyes. I had never seen her this way, never!

"I'm not going back! I quit!" she said tearfully.

I let her vent then I asked her what happened. She felt that the director was on her back, riding her too hard, and totally humiliating her. Her friends knew she was upset, and she told them that she quit. She wasn't going back.

After Ashley calmed down a little, I talked to her and reminded her how badly she wanted to be a color guard; and if she got out now, it would be difficult to get back in. It would be a shame for her to miss out on her goal because of what somebody else did. I told her that she should not let anyone keep her from her dreams, not to let someone else's actions determine what she does or does not do. I also gently reminded her that when we commit to do something, it is in good character to finish it. My parents always taught me that. "Your word is your bond and people should be able to depend on your word." Oh. Yeah. I didn't forget to mention the money I had also sacrificed to pay for this privilege. Ashley agreed with me and said that some of her friends had told her some of the same things.

Well, the next day, Ashley went to color guard practice; and her friends were happy to see her. The coaches looked at her and said, "They told us you weren't coming back."

She said, "Well, I'm here." Ashley had a fantastic year, wonderful experiences, and opportunities to travel. Look at what she would have missed if she didn't finish.

I imagine my point has not escaped you. I'm sure you get the moral of this story. So many times in life, we start things that we lay aside, walk away from, or just quit. Some of us feel like we are stifled; like we're not getting anywhere. May I suggest to you that the problem may be that you keep starting things that you don't finish. How many jobs have you had in five years? How many hobbies have you taken an interest in and never completed? How many committees have you volunteered for and showed up for one or two meetings? How many projects have you started but never completed? How many college courses have earned you a grade of incomplete? How many times have you said your family will have regular Bible study and prayer; and after three months, you can't remember the last time you had family prayer? And we wonder why our lives seem so *hodge-podge?*

Why is this issue of finishing what we start so important? It's simple. **Each completion is a stepping stone for the next round. When we are faithful in the small things, God entrusts us with larger things**—greater responsibilities because we've proven our faithfulness (Luke 16:10, 12; Matthew 25:14–29). The A&E channel is one of my favorites because it televises biographies of famous people. Almost every successful person featured started on a small scale. They did not scorn the small jobs or what may appear to be low level positions, and they completed what was necessary with a good attitude. They had many failures along the way, but they did not give up. Each time, this opened the door for something bigger. **Each completion builds experience and leads us on the path to our divine destiny.**

It's true that sometimes we can't finish because we are into something that God never told us to start in the first place. That's why it is so important to know God's voice. David said, "He leads me into paths of righteousness for his name sake" (Psalm 23:3). Remember this old familiar proverb? "Only one life. 'Twill soon be passed. Only what's done for Christ will last."

As Christians, everything that we do on earth should be with a heavenly mindset because in the end, what we did to promote the Kingdom of God is all that will really matter. Paul said that he willingly gave up everything in life, so that he might finish the course of his life with joy (Acts 20:24). Therefore, everything that we complete in our everyday living, God has a divine plan for it. Sometimes, we don't even realize how important the completion of the smallest of events or projects is until years later. Then we look back and understand why God had us do a certain thing at a certain period of time; or why we went through a particular circumstance or trial; so if we give up and don't persevere, we usually are affecting not only ourselves but generations that follow.

Let me remind you once again that we are created in the image of God. Go back to the Genesis records and you will observe that God did not stop creating the world until he had finished (Genesis 2:1–2). Look at Jesus. He proclaimed right up front to his mother, Mary, that he came to this earth for a purpose—to bring hope to the lost, to pay a price to bond mankind with God the Father, to die on a cross for the sins of the world (Luke 2:49). "Jesus said unto them. My meat is to do the will of him that sent me and to finish his work" (John 4:34, also see John 5:36). My friend, as Jesus hung on the cross of Calvary, he uttered the words, "It is finished" (John 19:30). Also, the Bible declares that the Holy Spirit who begins a good work in the regenerated heart of a person is able to complete it (Philippians 1:6). Just as the Father, Son, and Holy Spirit, we are to finish what we start.

Finishing a task brings a great sense of accomplishment. Not in a boastful way, but an assurance that you did what you were supposed to do in God's grand plan. Martin Luther King, Jr. had that experience. He knew that the fight for justice, equality, and brotherhood was not over; but he also knew that the part he had to play was done. Thus, in his last public speech, Dr. King compared himself to Moses with the words, "I've seen the promise land. I may not get there with you." He aligned himself with Paul, as he pronounced, "I would like to live a long life. Longevity has its place. But I'm not concerned about that now. I just want to do God's will." He knew he was going to die, but he left with the sense of *I finished.*

What about when we finally come to the end of our journey? Will we look back in regret and remember all the things we should have done? Or remember the things we brushed off and didn't even start because we thought they were too hard? Or will we joyfully join Martin Luther King, Jr. and Paul in saying, "I have fought a good fight. I have finished my course. I have kept the faith. Henceforth, there is laid up for me a crown of righteousness" (2 Timothy 4:7). Of course, I must remind you that in the race of life, the prize does not go to the fastest, but to those who finish (Matthew 24:13; Mark 13:13).

CHAPTER 10

SEEK GOD FIRST

October 15, 2003

Seek ye first the kingdom of God and his
righteousness, and all these things shall be
added unto you.

—Matthew 6:33

In the years when I was growing up, this was the most
preached message on a youth Sunday. While there are a
number of scriptures in the Bible directed strictly towards
children, I assure you that this is not one of them. In
context, Jesus speaks these words at the same time that
he teaches his disciples to pray. It is in the same chapter
that Christ tells us to store our treasures in heaven because
where our treasures are is where our heart will be. He goes
on to remind us that God takes care of the birds, trees,
flowers, and things of nature; so surely, he will take care of
his children. He instructs us not to worry about whether
or not we will eat, have a place to sleep, or survive. That

is what Jesus meant when he said, "All these things will be added unto you."

All the provisions that we need, God will provide them. This does not mean that they will drop out of the sky as manna dropped from heaven for the children of Israel as they wandered in the wilderness. It does mean that God is owner and controller of this universe, and the Holy Spirit works in the earth to make sure God's children have what they need. David said that he never saw the righteous forsaken or their children begging bread (Psalm 37:25). However, the first part of Jesus' statement is extremely important—seek God first. Please understand that God does not hold us hostage to his will. The framework and episodes of our lives are greatly dependent upon how much we submit our will and desires to God's will.

As I read that scripture, I'm reminded of the time that I was completing my undergraduate studies at the Bible college, Trinity International University. My eyes became more open to the truth of the Bible and to the fact that we have vast, unlimited resources available to us. I remember asking one of my professors a question. I observed that our grandparents and great-grandparents did not have all of these resources, but they seemed to be more committed and able to live by faith better than we do today. "Why is that?" I asked him.

I'll never forget his answer. It was simple, yet profound. He said, "They were more obedient."

For the most part, our ancestors just accepted God's Word as his Word. Whatever it took to put God first, they were willing to do. It's true that they did not always have a clear understanding in interpreting the Bible, and undue hardships that God never meant to happen were placed on them by leaders, but they were so willing to put God first that it didn't matter to them. Much of the undue hardship was because some were uneducated, but God saw their hearts and honored their faithfulness. Somehow, these uneducated people (with meager salaries) were able to build churches, establish communities, and even put children through college. Because they put God first, he met their needs. He also gradually led many of them away from man-made creeds and into the clearer understanding. As they learned the truth, they lived accordingly.

Now we have this thing that we are *seeking God's will for our lives*. His will is staring us right in the face, but we are still seeking. As Paul wrote to the Philippian Christians, this is because in reality, "Everyone seeks their own, not the things which are Jesus Christ's" (Philippians 2:21). You attend church every Sunday. You have gone to every seminar, listened to every taped message, and watched Christian TV networks day and night; but if you don't implement the principles that are taught, it does not change anything. Unlike our ancestors, we are not willing to do whatever it takes. We are not willing to suffer.

And then, instead of God, some are seeking a sign. Jesus told the Pharisees, "Why does this generation seek after a sign? I say unto you no sign shall be given to this generation" (Mark 8:12). God has given us his grace, his Word, and his Spirit. If we embrace these by faith, they are all we need to have intimacy with God and abundant life.

Then some seek Jesus, but only for what he can give them. Jesus told a group of people who were following him, "You seek me not because you saw miracles, but because you did eat of the loaves and were filled" (John 6:26). Think about it—if you were in relationship with someone, how would you feel if you realized that the person only wanted to be with you or around you because they want what you have? You're constantly doing for them, but they never think of you. We want people to like us for who we are, not for what they can get from us. God feels the same way. There is a song that says, "Lord, I praise you because of who you are, not for all the things that you have done."

God wants us to seek him first—before mother, father, children, spouse, friend, education, money, power, position, or anything. If we can just figure out that we don't lose anything by putting God first. After all, "He is a rewarder of those who diligently seek Him" (Hebrew 11:6).

CHAPTER 11

MY INSPIRATION

June 15, 2003
Revised April 29, 2018

The movie "Sarah, Plain and Tall" has a scene where the woman, Sarah, in a letter refers to her three aunts that raised her as *The Aunts*. When I heard this, it made me reflect on my own experience. After my sisters and I were full grown women, my mom and dad told us that when we were children, they made an agreement with each other that they would not interfere with any instructions and correction that our grandparents or aunts would give us (even if they didn't totally agree). They said that they knew our grandparents and aunts cared about us, and they wouldn't do anything to hurt us. Mom and Dad did not know it, but I believe they were simply following a long-term plan that God had mapped out for our lives. Although Mom and Dad taught us good manners, instilled a good work ethic, took us to church, and gave us tools for a good, productive, moral life, God used Grandma and *The Aunts* to plant spiritual seeds for future intense growth and magnification.

The Aunts had a powerful impact on us that will last a lifetime.

My parents always heard me say, "I want to be like Aunt Mary." They always assumed that I was just referring to her physical appearance, but it went deeper than that. First of all, I saw her as a strong woman (almost invincible) and an incredible lady. She seemed to be able to take care of anything, and I liked (for lack of a better phrase) her public relations gift. Aunt Mary could be chitterlings today and filet minion tomorrow. She could shop at the Goodwill store and find every bargain store and garage sale in town, yet give her best to those she loved. She could minister to the underdogs of society, yet conduct herself quite well in the midst of the elite. She was comfortable talking with the unwed mother, the Jewish friend, the White lady on the bus, or the president of a five-fortune company. She wasn't afraid to explore new cultures, and she wasn't so pretentious that she couldn't have a good time. In her everyday dealings with people, Aunt Mary never made them feel condemned. She joined Paul in her experience to be all things to all people without compromising the Gospel. However, she had the unique gift of blessing you out about one thing or another, and you walked away laughing. You just couldn't be mad at Aunt Mary; and to be honest, she couldn't be mad at you. Because she was noted for not holding her tongue, she told you what she had to say, and that was the end of it. She didn't hold anything in her heart, and her laugh was like none I've heard before or after. One couldn't help but be joyful around her. These things I admired in my Aunt Mary—my godmother. Now occasionally, you'll hear my sisters say to me, "Aunt Mary still lives." But she lives not only through me—**yes, in her only daughter, Leah. We all sit in awe as we observe Aunt Mary still dwelling among us**—in image, in speech, in spirit, and in all the qualities manifested through Leah.

In addition to being a church State Youth Director, visiting churches and conducting youth rallies, Aunt Mary was well known and respected in the Perrine Community (a Miami/Dade township). She would fellowship and preach in other churches in the community, showing the love of God. However, she also preached revivals in different Church of God of Prophecy (COGOP) locations. This is the name of the denomination of the Pentecostal church in which I grew up. Many times, she would pack my cousins, my sisters, and me in her car, and drive to her revival destination.

I'll never forget. I was eleven years old. Aunt Mary was the speaker at a revival in the Coconut Grove COGOP. The anointing of God was so powerful that night that I accepted Christ as my Savior.

My grandmother bore sixteen children and raised twelve. (Four died as babies.) Aunt Mary was the fourth child. When my grandfather died in 1959, Aunt Mary left college to return home and help my grandmother raise the seven youngest children. Her three older siblings (including my mother) were married and raising families of their own; and one younger brother was on his own also.

Because of her dedication to her vow to stick with my grandmother, Aunt Mary married in her mid-thirties. That was uncommon in that era. Her husband (Uncle George) was older and most of his children were adults. He had one young eight-year old son, whom Aunt Mary helped raise. They were married for many years, and Aunt Mary thought she could not conceive a child. However, at age forty-five, Aunt Mary learned she was pregnant. The doctors made all sorts of negative predictions. They said the baby would have Down syndrome and would be underdeveloped because of her age. They tried to convince her to have an abortion, but she was not even entertaining that thought. Her only daughter, Leah, was born with no birth defects. She is one of the most brilliant extraverts you will ever meet. Leah has always been clever, witty, and is now married with three young daughters of her own. Leah is also preaching the Gospel of Christ, just like her mother.

Aunt Mary discovered as an adult that she had Type 1 diabetes. This caused her many physical difficulties the last ten years of her life. However, it didn't keep her from loving Leah and pouring knowledge and wisdom into her young life. Sadly, as a nine-year old, Leah had to say goodbye to her best friend—her mother. Aunt Mary left Leah in the care of my Aunt Keturah and said, "Leah will be alright."

The circle was broken by Aunt Mary. She was the first of her siblings to pass away. However, I could write this without a tear because the memories are so rich. They only bring smiles. The last thing that Aunt Mary said to me as she lay on the hospital bed was, "Stay with God. Heaven is real." One of her favorite phrases was, "God didn't bring me this far to leave me." I believe she experienced the fullness of that statement as she glimpsed heaven from where she lay. At that point, there was no turning back to this world. Thank God for using Aunt Mary in my life. I'll never forget.

These are three of the *Aunt Mary* stories that continue to circulate my family decades later.

This Ain't No Picnic
(Words we'll always remember)

It was February 1988, and Grandma (my mom's mother) had died. The family would gather for the week at Aunt Martha's house. Friends and church family stopped by to offer condolences and bring food and drink. For many of us third generation family members, this was our first real loss or experience with death. So needless to say, it was quite a solemn occasion. One particular night, one of the young children of the family went into the kitchen and asked for something (can't remember what). A few seconds later, another one came. Then other children started parading to the kitchen.

Out of nowhere, Aunt Mary yells, "Wait a minute! This ain't no picnic!" Everyone burst out with laughter, and it has been a running joke in the family ever since. Occasionally, you'll hear some frustrated mother, aunt or cousin ring out with those infamous words, "This ain't no picnic!" Then we immediately think about Aunt Mary.

Welcome to the Family
(The Shelton Story)

I believe it was Thanksgiving 1988, in Grandma's backyard. Being one of the many great cooks of the family, Aunt Mary had succulently prepared the turkey, ham, POSSUM, and RACOON. (You can say it—YUCK!) Just picture it. The food has been blessed, and everyone is sitting around serving themselves or waiting to be served. Shelton (my sister's husband [fiancé at the time] and a native of Jacksonville) politely says, "Oh, no, thank you. I don't care to have any of that." Aunt Mary picks up a piece of possum and shoves it into his mouth and yells, "You young people got to learn how to survive!" Needless to say, Shelton was left surprised, stunned, and speechless. If Shelton didn't know the real Aunt Mary, he was introduced that day with his official welcome to the family.

You're No Professional
(The *Brown* Story)

This setting was the early 1990s in business meeting at the Perrine Church of God of Prophecy (the church established by my grandfather and where I attended as a child). I was not there but have heard the story told many times. The members of the church were discussing the issue of having an effective and adequate drum set. Aunt Mary was making some points about what was needed and why.

My dad (Leon Brown) stood and said, "I play the set we have now, and I don't see any problem with it." Aunt

Mary quickly replied in only a way that she can, "You're no professional!"

Everyone started laughing, including Aunt Mary and Dad. If you knew her, you just couldn't get mad at her. This is another one of those phrases that has survived time.

CHAPTER 12

THE 4 *R*'S

January 15, 2004

And if I have taken anything from any man by false accusation, I restore him fourfold.

—Luke 19:8b

Repentance—a change of mind, with sorrow, for something done, and a wish that it was undone.

Restitution—making good of or giving an equivalent for some injury; paying back for something taken from its rightful owner.

Restoration—bringing back to a former condition or position; reinstatement.

Reconciliation—to restore to friendship, harmony, or communion; adjust and settle differences.

Initially, I started out to write about *restitution*. However, my revelation was extended for complete understanding; and so we are here to discuss the **4 *R*'s: repentance, restitution, restoration, and reconciliation.**

The principle of restitution has existed almost as long as mankind has existed. The concept is that, if you take something that you have no legal right to, you must pay for it. We've heard the quote, "An eye for an eye, and a tooth for a tooth," (Exodus 21, 22; Leviticus 6:2–5, 24:18–21). Well, this entire concept is straight out of the Bible; and because it is grounded in Old Testament doctrine, many feel that it is not relevant for today's way of life. Therefore, in modern day Christianity, in most cases, this principle has been abandoned. However, this is a very relevant principle that God intends us to practice.

A small bit of evidence for my position is found in the New Testament (Luke 19). The short tax collector, Zacchaeus, ran after Jesus to tell him, "I will give half my wealth to the poor, and if I have taken anything from any man by false accusation, I restore him fourfold." This is not the amazing part of this event. The amazing part is that Jesus turned and said to the crowd, "This day has salvation come to this house forasmuch as he also is a son of Abraham." What Zacchaeus, in essence, did was confess his sins, and that he was willing to make his wrongs towards others right. He was willing to make restitution. Because of repentance and a right heart condition, Zacchaeus was saved.

Even without the example of Zacchaeus, I'd like to submit to you that God never intended the principle of restitution to be abandoned. The Old Testament rituals, laws, and events were established by God to help us understand the new covenant (New Testament). I agree that we no longer sacrifice animals for our sins because Jesus was the perfect Lamb of God who was slain once and for all at Calvary. Now, by believing in Jesus, our sins are cleansed.

I know I'm going the long way around, but please stay with me. Jesus said that the greatest law is that thou shall love the Lord thy God, and the second greatest law is to love thy neighbor as thyself. In other words, God cares most of all about our relationship with him. Then he cares about our relationship with each other. Follow me as I show you how God has taken each of the *4 R's* and wrapped them in the salvation process.

We were all born in sin because Adam (the first man) disobeyed God. In essence, he killed the spirit part of us and separated the human race from God. However, when we come to God and confess that we are sorry for our sins, this is **repentance.** At that time, we accept Christ as our Savior. Immediately, **restitution** is made because Christ already paid the price on Calvary for the sins that we committed against God. Immediately, our spirits are born again and **restored** to the state that God intended them to be (alive). Immediately, we are **reconciled** to God. We are now the friends of God and have the right to communicate with him. This happens supernaturally in a matter of seconds. This reconciles an individual to God. This takes care of our relationship with God.

Now remember, our relationship with each other is the second most important thing to God. Remember what Jesus told his disciples? "The world will know that you are my disciples by the love that you show towards each other" (John 13:34). We (Christians) are the natural models in the earth to demonstrate supernatural law. When people who don't know Christ begin to see repentance, restitution, restoration, and reconciliation operating among the people of God, it will draw them to God. Why do you think Jesus prayed before He went to the cross for God to make us one as he and the Father are one (John 17:21)? If there is offense and hurt among us, there can be no oneness. There can be no unity. That's why he left the model. He told us what to do. "If you bring your gift to the altar and remember that your brother has something against you, leave your sacrifice at the altar, and go and apologize and be reconciled to your brother [or sister], then come and offer your sacrifice to God" (Matthew 5:23–24).

The above is the formula for how Christians should be in relationship with each other. But when it comes to Christians operating with people outside the Kingdom of God, Jesus takes it to another whole level. Get this! "Love your enemies; bless them that curse you; do good to them that hate you; and pray for them that despitefully use you and persecute you that you may be the children of your Father which is in heaven" (Matthew 5:44). The bottom line is, as children of God, we must show love to everybody.

But if you are a part of the Kingdom of God, you have a duty to attempt to make your wrongs against others right.

Now, I've heard Christians say, "Once I get on my knees and talk to God about it, and he forgives me, that's all that matters." That's a lie straight from the ultimate deceiver (Satan). I just gave you the scripture where Jesus said to stop praying and go to the person and make it right. We are also instructed to confess our faults to one another and pray for each other so that we can be healed [restored] (James 5:16). The Bible says, if a person says [s]he loves God whom [s]he has not seen, but hates another human being whom [s]he can see, that person is a liar. It is a commandment that we love each other (1 John 4:20–21). When repentance and confession have taken place, then that is the time for both parties to rush to prayer to worship the God who gives us the willingness and ability to repent and forgive.

Therefore, when my brother [sister] comes to me sorrowful about something [s]he has done to me, I then forgive him/her. If the offense is something that can be made right or given back (or paid back) in some way, then that needs to happen. If it cannot be done, then the apology must stand in place of the restitution and restoration. Reconciliation may be hindered by our human nature; but by God's grace, reconciliation can be processed and achieved. Remember that it is the Holy Spirit working through us that enables this to happen. That's why it is going to seem strange, weird, and peculiar to non-Christians. But if they see this happening as often as it should, they will be drawn to the God who is making it all happen.

Please understand that making restitution does not always mean that you will not suffer the consequences of your actions. Sometimes, God, in His mercy, will allow consequences to be avoided; and sometimes, he won't.

CHAPTER 13

FORGIVENESS

The Missing Link
February 29, 2004

Offended's Part

Forgiveness

Repentance &
Restitution

Restoration &
Reconciliation

Offender's Part   God's Part

But when you pray, first forgive anyone
you are holding a grudge against so that
your Father in heaven will forgive you
your sins too.

—Mark 11:25 (Living Bible)

In the previous chapter, I wrote that repentance, restitution, restoration, and reconciliation were all wrapped up in the plan of salvation. We learned that the salvation conversion takes a matter of seconds. There is only one thing that makes this possible—upon repentance, God immediately forgives us, which kicks into play the remaining *R*s. Remember, the Bible declares that, "A broken and contrite heart, God will not despise" (Psalm 57:17). God is faithful and just to forgive us our sins (1 John 1:9) This all has to do with our being reconciled to God.

Now remember, the second most important thing to God is our relationship with each other. In this much slower model of God's grace, the duty falls upon the offender to repent of his deeds toward another person and make restitution. Restoration and reconciliation are brought by God himself; but before God's two pieces of the puzzle can be put into place, something else has to happen—**the offended must forgive the offender. This is the missing piece. This is the part that people think they can overlook and still be content and have the peace of God.** In the Lord's Prayer printed in Matthew 6, Jesus prayed to God the Father. "Forgive us as we forgive those who trespass against us." The inference is that as we forgive others, God will forgive us. In fact, in Biblical recordings, Jesus boldly states that if we don't forgive others, God will not forgive us (Matthew 6:15; Mark 11:25–26; Luke 6:36–37).

Some will try to make excuses and say, "Well, God didn't mean this, or God didn't mean that, or God doesn't expect so-and-so." You know, God speaks very clearly; but we sometimes refuse to listen. Peter asked Jesus, "How many times should I forgive my brother?" Jesus answered him in a way that I'm almost sure Peter wasn't expecting. Jesus said forgive your brother seventy times seven [in one day implied—see Luke 17:3] (Matthew 18:21). That's 490 times in one day. That statement leaves no room for diverse interpretation, and either you accept it or you don't. Read the entire chapter of Matthew 18 where Jesus tells a story to emphasize this principle.

Now, does that mean that we should intentionally put ourselves in harm's way? No, if we know that someone does not have our best interest at heart or is intentionally out to get us, then we should stay clear of that person. Jesus did this many times during his ministry. He fled for his life because the time had not yet come for him to die, and he knew certain people wanted to harm him. Yet, as he hung on the cross dying, he could extend forgiveness to his murderers—"Father, forgive them for they know not what they do" (Luke 23:34). Right now, someone is saying, "That's all fine and good. He's God. I'm human."

Yes, you are human, with the Spirit of God deposited inside of you. He is the enabling power. If we are not walking in the Spirit, forgiveness is virtually impossible. But, remember that the Spirit of God produces the fruit of meekness, gentleness, longsuffering, and love. These are the treasures of God that yield the power to forgive.

Now, I must caution here that forgiveness is not pretending that the offense never happened and continuing to allow the offender to do the same thing over and over again. This helps no one. So when Jesus told us to forgive 490 times in one day, he does not mean to say nothing and just let the person keep going on like nothing ever happened. As a matter of fact, it is our duty to let the offender know that we are offended. There is a scripture in the Bible that says, "If a brother [sister] sins against you, go to him privately and confront him with his fault. If he listens and confesses it, you have won back a brother [sister]. But if not, then take one or two others with you and go back to him again, proving everything you say by these witnesses" (Matthew 18:15–16, Living Bible). I am warning you! "Rebuke your brother [sister] if he sins, and forgive him if he is sorry" (Luke 17:3, Living Bible).

Of course, the offender usually knows he wronged you; but the point is to let him/her know that you expect the offense to stop, then you have every right to separate yourself from the offender. Does this release you from having to forgive him/her? No, as a matter of fact, we have to walk in forgiveness even if the person has not repented. That is what Jesus did for us at the cross. Forgiveness for all mankind was granted at the time of Jesus' death on the cross. Therefore, when a person repents of his/her sins, forgiveness is readily available because it's always been there; and so it should be with us. Even though we separate ourselves from the situation, forgiveness is settled in our hearts. So when the offender finally says he/she is sorry, forgiveness is more easily granted because it has always been there.

Now, I'm not an idealist. I know that this is more easily said than done; but I also know that it is not impossible. It takes a close relationship with God through prayer. I also know that forgiveness is just as vital for the offended person as it is for the offender. Because when we don't forgive, we keep ourselves in unnecessary bondage; we keep blessings from flowing in our lives; we pass down resentment to our children; and curses continue for generations (Luke 6:38).

I think this old familiar hymn puts things into perspective:

> What a friend we have in Jesus;
> All our sins and grief to bear.
> What a privilege to carry everything to
> God in prayer.
> Oh, what peace we often forfeit;
> Oh what needless pains we bear;
> All because we do not carry everything to
> God in prayer.

CHAPTER 14

PEACE IN THE VALLEY

Coping with Life's Circumstances

June 15, 2003
Revised May 1, 2018

A newborn baby enters the world; a young person graduates from high school; the long-awaited promotion is approved; you walk down the aisle with the person of your dreams; you have the big house, money in the bank, and are living the American dream. It sounds good, doesn't it? Who couldn't be happy and worry-free in any of these situations. But what about when things aren't so good? Life just isn't going your way? Loved ones die; your child has a debilitating disease; you or your spouse are laid off a job; your neighbor hates you, and you don't even know why; your children have rejected God and gone their own way; instead of helping you, your church family gossips about you. Your world seems like it's falling apart. How can anyone be happy and worry-free in these kinds of situations? Well, I have found it very helpful to follow the advice and example of St. Paul. He said he learned to be content in whatever state he found himself. Sometimes, he had much and life was going great; and sometimes, he had very little and was at death's door. But he realized that there would be good times, and there would be bad. He was able to bear it because he knew he could do all things through Jesus Christ (Philippians 4:11–13).

I can hear some of you now saying, "Good for Paul. What about now in the real world?" I think we forget that the people we read about in the Bible were real people just like us; and in many cases, went through a lot more difficulty than we will ever experience. How many of us have found ourselves in jail unjustly? Paul found himself in that situation many times; yet he could write, "Rejoice in the Lord always . . . Be careful for nothing, but in everything by prayer and supplication with thanksgiving, let your request be made known unto God. **And the peace of God which passeth all understanding shall keep your hearts and minds through Jesus Christ**" (Philippians 4:4–7). Later in the same chapter in the Bible, Paul expresses his belief that God will supply all of his needs. I encourage you to read the entire chapter of Philippians 4. And if you're looking for examples you can relate to, remember that special person in your life who has survived and thrived through difficult times. I think of my mom, my Grandma Kemp, my Aunt Mary, and my Aunt Martha. They thanked God every step of the way through every trial. Aunt Martha used to say, "What are you doing under the circumstances? Get from under there and get under the blood of Jesus." My grandma lived thirty years as a widow and raised her last seven children and three grandchildren. However, she always extended help to others, moved forward, and worshiped and praised God. These women were great examples for me.

Are you getting it yet? We could have (and should have) the Peace of God, no matter what is happening in our lives. King David said, "Even though I walk through the darkest valley, I will fear no evil, for you [God] are with me" (Psalm 23:4, NIV). David had the Peace of God.

When Jesus was getting ready to go to the cross and leave earth, he said to his disciples, "Peace, I leave with you. My Peace I give unto you; not as the world giveth, give I unto you. Let not your heart be troubled, neither let it be afraid" (John 14:27). Jesus is saying those same words to us today.

It is important to realize that before we can have the Peace of God, we must have Peace with God. Throughout the Bible, the Gospel of Jesus Christ is consistently referred to as the Gospel of Peace (Ephesians 6:15). That is because Christ's death on the cross and resurrection restored peace between God and the human race. That's why he is called the Prince of Peace (Isaiah 9:6). So when we make Peace with God, we have gone through the salvation process (Romans 5:1). Then we are instructed to live in the Holy Spirit, and we will begin to develop Spiritual character. One of those character traits is the Peace of God (Galatians 5:22).

I'll admit that this is not something that happens overnight. So how do we develop the Peace of God? Become spiritually minded (Romans 8:6–18) Let your mind be filled with things that are true, honest, just, pure, virtuous, and praise worthy (Philippians 4:8). Have a thankful heart, practice doing what you read in the Bible, read psalms, and sing hymns and spiritual songs (Colossians 3:15–17). This is not something I'm making up. Go to the Bible and read it for yourself.

Why is it so important to have the Peace of God? Well, James told us that the trying of our faith creates patience, which builds our character (James 1:2–4). Paul said that our troubles build patience, and patience builds experience, and experience gives us hope (Romans 5:3–5). In Paul's words, "I consider that our present sufferings are not worth comparing with the glory that will be revealed in us" (Romans 8:18, NIV). But if we don't have the Peace of God, this process will not happen.

So does this mean we will never cry or show our emotions? Absolutely not. It does mean, once we have gone through the grieving process or gotten over the initial shock, we lay it down and move on. It does mean that we don't become hysterical for every little situation life brings, or linger in self-pity, or stay up all night worrying about things we can't change. I leave you with the words of Jesus. "These things I have spoken unto you, that in me ye might have peace. **In the world you shall have tribulation, but be of good cheer; I have overcome the world**" (John 16:33). Now, go in peace—The Peace of God.

CHAPTER 15

THE *ABSOLUTE* GOD

Jehovah God Was, Is, and Is to Come
September 15, 2003

It only takes a glimpse of the past forty years of American history to understand that our nation has gradually peeled away the spiritual truths upon which our country was built. Now, it is common place to find disgruntled citizens waving the star-spangled banner and the Constitution to justify banning the display of the Ten Commandments on public buildings or forbidding prayer at a graduation ceremony. Let's face it. It's not words on a building that are upsetting people. It is God himself. They have an issue with God.

Since the sexual and moral revolution of the 1960s, many Americans have lived on the slippery slope of, "If it feels good, do it," "I am my own man or woman," and "Tolerance is a virtue." Let's be honest. These are all smoke screens because human beings would rather walk in darkness than in light (John 3:19). In the New Testament, Paul explains that the entire purpose of the law (the Word of God) was so that humans could see our faultiness and sinful nature. It was our teacher to bring us to Christ (Galatians 3:1–29). The Apostle James uses the analogy that the law is like a mirror. When we look, we see ourselves; and a wise man will take the necessary steps to change what does not look right. So the law was never intended to save us—just to make us understand that we need God (James 1:22–25). Therefore, don't be astonished when there is a growing move to abolish the Ten Commandments or obliterate the mention of the name of Jesus Christ. People don't want to see their sin. They rather continue to deceive themselves. They don't want to look in the mirror because then they might have to change.

Did you know that the Bible also says that deep inside every man rests the knowledge of God (Romans 1:19)? Yes, so we may conclude that there is no such thing as an atheist. Every person knows that there is a God, but not every person wants to submit to God. That is why people fight so hard against the truth. As human beings, if we admit there is a God, then we may have to concede our own imperfections and the reality of Jesus. He's really the real problem, you know. You can talk about Buddah or meditation ceremonies. You can engage in a conversation about Mohamed and rituals of Islam. You can even pass the time listening to the traditions of Judaism. But don't you dare mention the name of Jesus. But the Bible already told us that Jesus would be a stumbling block and rock of offence to those who don't want to believe (Isaiah 8:14 and 1 Peter 2:8).

So what have we created here for ourselves in America? A place where every man does what is right in his own eyes (Judges 17:6). In our social thinking, there are no absolutes. What is wrong for me may not necessarily be wrong for you. I'll admit that there are some circumstances where this thesis can be applied; but it does not apply to what God mapped out from the first time he said, "Let us make man." The structure of nature changes; people change; fashions and styles change; centuries roll by; but **God does not change.** He is the same yesterday, today, and forever (Hebrews 13:8). He is Alpha and Omega. He was, is, and is to come (Revelations 1:8). In other words, he existed before the world existed; and he will exist when the world ceases to exist. God's Word is him; and he said heaven and earth will pass away, but the Word of God will never pass away. (Matthew 24:35). Therefore, people can remove the Ten Commandments from buildings, but they will never eliminate God or his Word.

I know that our minds cannot comprehend the full scale of who God is or his plan for the world; but John tells us that the Word (who is God) put on flesh and came to live in the presence of mankind (John 1:1–14). There was a purpose for this. He came to fulfill the law, not abolish it (Romans 8:3–5). All the rituals, traditions, history, and prophecy of the Old Testament would all culminate in the death and resurrection of Jesus Christ. Take some time to examine the Jewish sacrificial system, circumcision, exodus of a chosen people out of the land of Egypt with a promise of a new land, the lifting up of a serpent for healing, burial of a man in the belly of a fish for three days, and so much more. You will find that everything in the Old Testament points to a pivotal event—the coming of the Savior, Jesus Christ—and he plainly stated that he came to fulfill the law (Matthew 5:17).

It is hard for people who do not know God as Savior to understand the absoluteness of his Word because they read only for logical understanding instead of by a renewed spirit through Jesus Christ (1 Corinthians 1:19–21 and 2 Corinthians 2:9–16). Jesus further stated that he is the way, the truth, and the life. No person could have any communication or connection with the only true God, unless he believes that Jesus Christ is the Savior of the world (John 14:6). This is now considered to be an *intolerant* message. It is said that we are to *live and let live*. I agree that we should not be obnoxious in our approach; but we cannot allow our family, friends, and acquaintances to think that it does not matter how you come to God, as long as you acknowledge him. If we do this, we do not love people. It is not a popular message today; but popular or not, Jesus is the only way to God. If He's not, let's just throw away the Bible and forget this whole thing. I wasn't the first to make this statement. Paul said the same thing when he was preaching to the Corinthian Christians (1 Corinthians 15:12–19).

I'll agree—this is a shaky world that we live in. That is why our hope should not be in the things of this world; not even in our loved ones—they will fail us, too. There is no guarantee that our jobs will be waiting for us tomorrow, or that our husbands or wives will be faithful 'til death, or that our children will remember us in our aging years.

Hurricanes and floods yield unwarned upheaval every day. Life is flimsy. But in a changing, unpredictable world, I want future generations to know that when everything else in life is crumbling, we can hold to and rest in the unchanging, everlasting, absolute God.

Part 2

Three months after I wrote this reflection, I conducted a search on the word *absolute*. How awesome it is to know that all of these terms apply to the God of the universe. Truly something to ponder:

Absolute

Pure

Perfect   Complete   Sure

Faultless

Entire   Whole

Unblemished

Definite   Unmixed   Certain

Unlimited   Firm

Supreme   Positive

Ideal

Undeniable   Untarnished

ABOUT THE AUTHOR

Mareshah Brown Miller finds great rewards educating children in the Orange County Public Schools for more than twenty years. She previously enjoyed a successful twenty two-year career as a real estate/litigation paralegal in a few Miami-Dade County law firms. With her bachelor's Degree in Human Resource Management and Master's Degree in English Education, she has been afforded opportunities to communicate in various platforms. Growing up in the suburbs of Miami, Florida among a large close-knit family and rich spiritual training has helped Miller develop a candid and inviting writing style. Among other descriptions, she is a daughter, wife, mother, sister, aunt, neighbor, and friend. Her personal essays are shaped by her life experiences and reveal an innate desire to encourage and inspire others. *Divine Pearls* is a collection of personal and intimate short stories in which the author uniquely weaves spiritual revelation, inspiration, and encouragement.